JUDGE MY HOUSE

Destiny of a Bloodline

by

SHERI SCOTT

Illustrations by
Karalyn Kohan

JUDGE MY HOUSE: Destiny of a Bloodline
Copyright ©2020 by Sheri Scott
Illustrations ©2019 by Karalyn Kohan
Book design ©2020 by Integrates Marketing
All rights reserved.

No part of this book may be used or reproduced in any manner whatsoever, or stored in a retrieval system, or transmitted in any form or by any means, electronic, mechanical, photocopying or otherwise, without written permission except in the case of brief quotations embodied in critical articles and reviews.
For information, address:
Published by : SHAREalike
An Imprint of SHARE Publishing
A division of Share Resources Inc.
Calgary, Alberta, Canada.
www.shareresourcesinc.com

ISBN 978-1-989269-38-1 (paperback)
ISBN 978-1-989269-39-8 (ebook .epub)
First Edition

JUDGE MY HOUSE

Destiny of a Bloodline

DEDICATION

I am dedicating this book to the Spirit of the Lord. I don't have much to say other than thank you, I am grateful, honoured and humbled to be taught by you.

INTRODUCTION

This concept of judging my house has been an interesting, unfolding and expanding revelation that has brought a lot of freedom from things ruling my being, my life and my choices, that otherwise perplexed me.

Most of this book is from posts I have made over the years in Terry Spencer's Courtrooms of Heaven Facebook group. I am so thankful for this group and the experiences and understanding everyone shares in there. The group has grown dramatically over the years I have been a member and through that growth, our Father showed me that He is bringing people into heaven in an ever-increasing number. The breadth of experience is so beneficial and also the breadth of trials and suffering have had a dramatic impact on me.

When I began to realize that judgement from our Father is a way out of the captivity of the rulers of this world - I had a renewed hope like never before. My first experience of being judged under the blood of Yeshua was really painful and terrifying, until He smiled and showed me the judgment scroll. It said, Paid in Full. This is Christianity 101, the provision of forgiveness of sin.

I was shocked at this simple truth after being a Christian for so many years, I knew it but I didn't know it like this.

Because this book is a compilation of posts I have made and things I have tried to explain in the group in conversation with others, I have attempted to categorize them by topic. My express hope in publishing this is that we are reminded of who He is, who we are, and that we desire to understand the structure and function of justice and judgement. It matters that we can render a righteous judgement. It matters that we are untethered from the rulers of this world. It matters that we are sanctified by Him, made Holy as He is Holy, and that we learn how to operate within our Father's kingdom. To come out and be separate, and be about our Father's business.

I am so thankful for Terry Spencer and his transparent journey and willingness to share his revelation with us in humility. The Courtrooms of Heaven Facebook group has spun off regional COH Facebook groups, mobilized legislators, started courses and training sessions, webinars, a YouTube channel, pop-up zoom discussions, several new governing and creating Facebook groups, and has maintained a collection of resources from a variety of people.

Terry Spencer and Nina Hayden have a new book as well called Governing Creation from the Courts of Heaven. www.revolutionglory.com

Although I am stringing together posts from a Facebook group, my hope is that it will all thread together to paint a picture of having our house judged. That we can come to love what He loves and hate what He hates, because we are aligning with our Father YHVH, His son YHSVH and His Spirit, Ruach HaKodesh. That more and more we reflect the image we are created in, and we position our bloodlines into his likeness and purpose, and align the destiny of our bloodline.

Table of Contents

1. Judgement as Provision - Father

   11
2. Blood as Provision - Son

   17
3. Counsel as Provision - Holy Spirit

   23
4. Our Advocate - Yeshua

   29
5. Witness Stand - Seen and Unseen Testimony

   35
6. Foreign Governments - Complicit Bloodlines

   45
7. Transfer of Rulership - Overcome the World

   73
8. Going Forward

   91

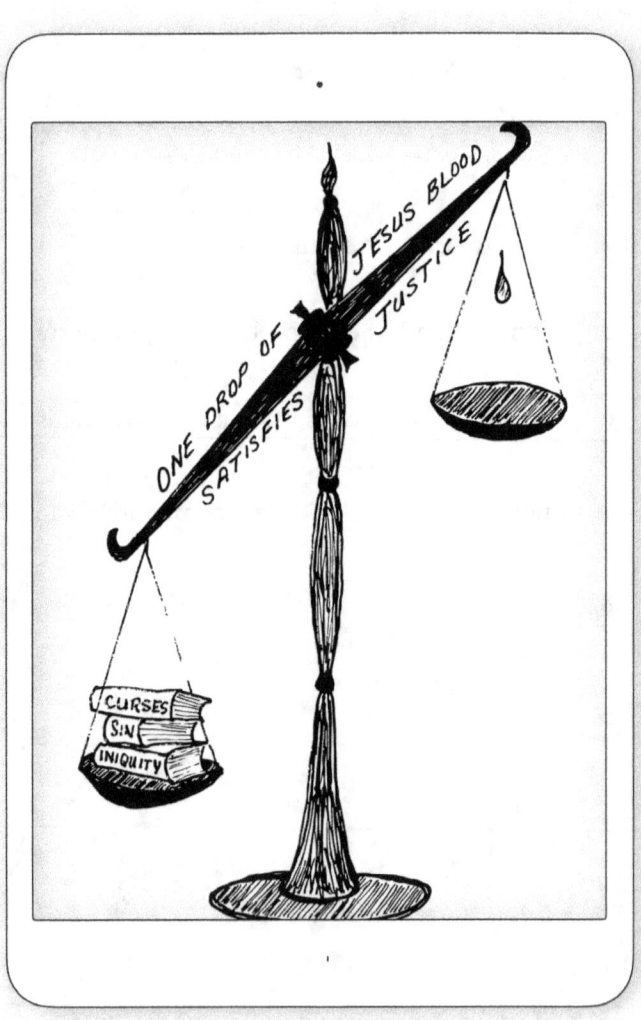

CHAPTER ONE
Judgement is Provision - Father

Something that I've noticed in my own personal untangling, sanctifying and redeeming is that things can get messy. I think a few things come into play when we are evaluating what we see, dream and encounter. There is a measure of resistance in 'coming out from under' another government, a kingdom of this world, being influenced by other spirits or 'rulers'.

We tend to process information and experiences within a framework of understanding. The whole framework may be wrong - yet, it is the only way we know. So, the key objective is connecting closer with the Trinity. Otherwise we can be led astray or deceived or kept from Truth. We can be kept out of heavenly realms and remaining in realms of the spirit that are the wrong kingdom with the wrong courtrooms.

Judgement from our Father is our provision and it is a safe place. The blood of Jesus is our covering and is also a safe place, as is the name of the lord, YHVH. The righteous run into it and are safe. We are typically unaware of lies that have become our refuge because they can be pre-existing mindsets we 'resonate' with since birth. We don't know what we don't know, and resonating with something doesn't mean it is good.

I have had the old 'idea' that my communication with my Father is, or needs to be in prophetic riddles, judged under the blood of Jesus. I ask Him to judge my neural pathways and stored record of iniquity and belief systems and lies, and to redeem my thinking and my understanding, including my understanding of Him.

We tend to operate on a 'this means that' framework and it is part of the ungodly governance of religion. It is a way to 'understand' apart from talking with Jesus and getting understanding from him. It actually keeps us away from him and instead, seeking a substitute of information or knowledge. I love the scripture that says, in all your getting, get understanding. We need to ask for judgement of what we are 'standing under' and re-align our 'standing' to 'under' the headship of Jesus, and the government of our Father.

We will see and encounter some strange things in other realms. We can have our 'fear' of the unknown judged along with a 'false sense of safety', under the blood of Jesus. We need this dealt with because we have not been this way before. There is a ditch on both sides of the road, fearing the unknown and a false sense of safety in what we think we know. I have found this no longer means that, it might mean five different things I never knew or thought of before. YET, we are told in scripture, you need not that any man teach you but I myself will teach you by my Holy Spirit. We are led and guided into all Truth, and Jesus is the Truth. Judgement divides and demolishes, we take thoughts captive when we bring them into court along with encounters, experiences, dreams and visions too.

2 Corinthians 10:5 We demolish arguments and every pretension that sets itself up against the knowledge of God, and we take captive every thought to make it obedient to Christ.

I have heard many say that court in heaven is a tool. I understand this usage of the term tool as it is the 'means'. What we are really doing by engaging in anything in court in heaven is receiving justice and judgement, these are 'provisions' for us from our Father. We are bringing our lives under the blood. We are administrating His kingdom. So, it seems odd to call that a tool, in this light. We should desire this provision for ourselves, our bloodlines and the world, as it is the 'process' of receiving our redemption that Jesus paid for.

Otherwise, what do we think His blood covers us from? The enemy? There is a teacher who mentions on a podcast that an angel explained the judicial system in heaven to him as being created from our Father's laughter. He who sits in the heavens laughs. This is so very awesome to comprehend. I consider it aligning when I too can laugh.

Going to our Father as our judge, is to receive His provision of judgement for us. It cleanses us of unrighteousness. One of the provisions of the blood of Jesus is to cover us to withstand this judgement. So, when we confess and ask to be judged under the blood, what remains is purified and made Holy as He is holy. When any accusation is coming forth (brought into light, spoken, thought or felt) that you are: assuming, wrong, right but self-righteous, or self-elevated etc., you can bring that accusation into court and as a priest on behalf of your bloodline and plead guilty, receive judgement under blood, receive forgiveness and carry on. It doesn't change your rightness or wrongness, but it will purify any hidden pride about your rightness or wrongness. I personally welcome these types of 'overt' feedback or accusations as they are intended for my purification, which I love.

Many want to go to the throne room or the throne of grace so to clarify, the throne room in heaven as described in scripture, is not the same as a courtroom, (mobile court of accusation and the kingdom realms), Our Father's throne with righteousness and justice as it's foundations, IS the ruling authority that is manifested through the system. They are in different realms altogether. There are other courts within the different kingdom realms, (kingdom of God, kingdom of heaven, kingdom of the earth) as well. Once we are accessing the different courts and realms, it becomes clearer as to 'where' we are. This is our personal maturing into lordship, kingship and judgeship. It is legislative and judicial.

I have also found functioning as a priest can be done here too, when acting on behalf of other people before our Father. When functioning as a priest the other direction, from our Father to man, it's very different! I am clarifying the 'geography' for lack of a better word. The throne room has nothing unclean in it yet the mobile court or court of accusation can, simply on the basis of where it is located. It's convened out of a kingdom realm that overlays satan's realms so people often get confused. It is not a different perspective but a literal different place.

In regard to this location, my advice is never to ask the enemy what you are accused of as this is not your source of truth. Always let Jesus, your advocate and Holy Spirit, your counsellor reveal this to you as your source of Truth.

CHAPTER TWO
Blood is Provision - Son

Bob Jones - Shepherd's Rod 1998 (can be found on his website):
"The first way to turn back God's judgments is through repentance. After repentance, we then go to the courts of God to file charges against the evil that is being released to bring devastation on the earth. In essence, we are going to the Lord's courthouse in order to file charges, or to plead our case, not on the basis of our righteousness, but by His blood."

Regarding Bob's statement, I believe confession is a guilty plea. I think it's great that the courtroom 'how to' teaching is lacking in the sense that all of our relationships are unique. Mobile court is at the heart of migrating our lives under the blood and headship of Jesus. If you aren't asking him 'how to', start there. We should be able to glean from others, as our counsellor highlights truths to us, yet our counsellor is also our teacher and therefore who we learn from.

We create and we are our own pathways in heavenly realms. I personally would connect with Jesus first in my heart, and we would go together from there. Pathways get more direct as they get established which means, I can access instantly and so will you be able to. The ability to see gets clearer the more you engage. I feel and sense more than I see, often I don't recognize or grasp what I am seeing anyway as many things are new and don't look like or appear like anything I have seen before.

Mobile court looks like any or most courtrooms on earth to me. Jesus took me there the first time and from engaging with Him, we were instantly there. It was not like linear travel. Mobile court of accusation is always available for you and you can pause and re-engage anytime. It is not in an earthly time realm and so it doesn't function in linear time. I would often pop in to court while driving around doing errands, with my eyes open, being in both realms at same time, seeing both realms like an overlay.

I find communication in heavenly realms is more along the lines of thinking at or with each other, knowing things as if they were spoken. There is spoken word as well but it is lesser communication as it doesn't bring the fullness of infused understanding.

Many are coming from an intercession framework of understanding and purpose yet I suggest first, we bring our own junk in to get judged, brought under the provision of the blood. Then we move on to petitioning on behalf of others, issues, circumstances, concerns and mandates. This back and forth of dealing with ourselves and others, continues at deeper levels and we must have clean hands and a pure heart. Anything that is circumventing dealing with yourself first, is usually a wrong trade. It puts a protocol or a system above your personal relationship with Jesus and his blood. For example, we can be avoiding intimacy with Jesus because of wanting to feel important, self-exaltation in spiritual things, manipulation regarding outcomes and trading with ungodly governments to get our needs met.

You can be 'in the spirit' and not in the kingdom of God, that is why establishing a pathway for yourself with Jesus is crucial. Many are accessing shadow courts and have bizarre encounters there, and have no idea they are NOT in our Father's kingdom realm. We need to be clear that our image centre is where we process our sight, our imagination and it needs to be judged also.

I would question any vision or encounter with anything ungodly presenting as 'okay' or 'acceptable' and we have safeguards.

1) If you are always with Jesus in any given realm, you are good to go.

2) You can take any encounter, vision or dream into court to have it judged under the blood. This will remove anything not of Him.

3) If you are with Jesus and still having ungodly encounters, this is a sticking point. You will want to question everything, and it may be unsettling. This is where you need to settle issues of righteousness with Jesus. It's work to get here but is required.

I have no idea why during biblical sacrifices, the altar had an area to catch the blood so it didn't go into the land. The other gods or godlings had requirements that the blood of their sacrifices was to intentionally drip into the land and the water. There is so much about blood that we don't know yet and it continues to be an unraveling mystery. What I do know is that the blood of Jesus ran into the earth and the earth around there opened and the dead came out and walked around the city. That is powerful. That is life, redemption, safety, pure, powerful, reviving and the resurrection!

The idea that this same blood testifies on our behalf means that everything in our blood (DNA record of iniquity) has been redeemed. Our blood aligns when covered by Jesus' blood, this is the covering we are intended to have. The religious government has sold a big lie that your pastor or church is your covering. A religious spirit wants to cover you because it means you become its slave, and maybe has been your covering, but like all things Jesus redeemed us from with his very lifeblood, all false coverings get to be judged by the true covering.

When I realized that I have the provision of Jesus' blood to cover me (I know this seems basic), I then also realized every 'other' spiritual government that has ruled aspects my life and being, stealing, killing and destroying - does not get this provision. So, I do ask for it to also be judged with the same judgement I am receiving. Ever heard people use the term 'plead the blood'? That terminology has been so disempowered from the reality, that it is used mostly as a religious trade to appease fear. The power is in the reality that my only defense is Yeshua and him crucified, his blood. So, I recognize that everything is under his blood, I take specific action to have other coverings, including the sin and iniquity covering judged. I come in to agreement with one head and one covering only, His. I can honestly say that these simple truths are so ever expanding that I can delight in the simplicity and realize I was only understanding a small fraction.

Every foreign satanic governmental being has to answer to our Father and the blood compels it to. We could call the mobile court of accusation the Blood Court.

Isaiah 1:18 says...

"Come now, let us reason together, says the Lord: though your sins are like scarlet, they shall be as white as snow; though they are red like crimson, they shall become like wool."

Or in other words, made like him.

There is so much that can be said about the blood as our provision but I think it's a good start to see that it is what allows us to have our house judged. Otherwise, we would be dead, as his judgements are righteous and true.

CHAPTER THREE
Counsel is Provision - Holy Spirit

I just went to the courthouse to file a claim yesterday, in my city. The Law Society provides services for free on the main floor. They are administrators and tell you what paperwork you need, how to fill it out, how many copies you need, how to serve the other party and what court to file your papers in. They walk you through the process but don't offer legal advice. They advise on the process only as well as swear affidavits for you.

On the 15th floor is a whole group of volunteer lawyers offering free legal advice. Obviously for smaller issues where it is not feasible to hire a lawyer. They can tell you what to say, what not to say, and exactly what you should be looking to accomplish, and what you can expect. They advise on the law and strategy.

It demystifies the whole process to have some information and support. I have noticed the exact parallel with the mobile court.

There is protocol, so the same claims are made by different people. The same hearing and court proceedings happen with a handful of variables. A decision is made, recorded and varying methods of enforcement are standard procedure. Jesus, as my lawyer, and I go to court and he teaches me 'live', yet I love gleaning the information from the experiences that others have.

I was explaining 'why' the process of entering a plea, being judged and obtaining a 'divorce' in heavenly court is necessary to a friend the other day and I reduced it down to the simplicity of this: I am marrying Jesus, I need to be divorced from any other ruling entities. Legally, I can't marry Him if I am still married through my bloodline to any other entity. It seemed so simple when I said it. It is the same as citizenship, allegiance, slavery - If I am a citizen of heaven, I need to 'not' be a citizen of this world, having an allegiance to another kingdom. With regards to slavery, scripture is clear that Jesus 'purchased' us. That means we were owned as a slave by someone else. We have a previous owner, a spiritual entity, though many don't recognize this as trafficking, we were being held captive and have been freed. Now, as we judge our religious covering, the scales fall from our eyes and we are beginning to see the extent of this. This requires a very specific order of unfolding truth in our understanding and Holy Spirit is so delicate with us in showing us painful hard truths. Comforter, counsellor and friend.

We require permission to do and ask certain things even if we know we are able. Sometimes our permission is scripture itself, as a framework. Holy Spirit usually brings to mind the scriptures I need in the moment when I am seeking what to do about a particular issue or circumstance. For example, if I am asking for something on behalf of someone else, there are scriptures that show that I am permitted such as, authority for families, husband and wife become one, a nation is a bloodline and nations are Jesus' inheritance. Asking Holy Spirit for guidance needs to be seamless in everything we do. This is how we begin to recognize how little we ask and how much we lean on our own understanding.

An example of being 'other governed' in business would be deals that don't deal. It can be like the eleventh hour and it turns sour or goes sideways or drops off the table completely. An example of this pattern in certain areas in business, is like a project to be funded that you have a contract on and the funding deal falls through and you don't get the contract as a result. It is a third-party responsibility, but you suffer the trickle-down effects.

My recommendation would be to take the deal and funding and outflow of the deal being funded (ex: contracts and commitments) and ask for the whole package and everyone involved to be judged under the blood. Then ask to be separated from any ungodly agreements you may be about to enter into that you can't see. By submitting the whole package, you are in essence saying "God, if you aren't in this deal, I'm not doing it - even if the funding is begging me to". This includes judging everything you have thought was God or from God or divinely 'set-up' such as expectations, fears, whether anyone else thought God was in it or your motives were pure. Judgement under the blood is a safety provision for us. Jesus our attorney and Holy Spirit our counsellor, are happy to inform us of other undealt with legal rights and issues.

There is a scripture in proverbs that says the prudent sees danger and seeks refuge yet the simple keeps going and suffers for it. Similarly, is the one about pride coming before a fall. We have the personal availability to have counsel on matters we need to know about. Even the simplest things like what people call a check in their spirit about a decision. This is our wise counsellor working out what is best for us - when we aren't even asking. Then we need to deal with why we don't even ask. I have way too many examples of this foolish way of living and we are picking them off with judgement one at a time!

CHAPTER FOUR
Our Advocate - Yeshua

I regularly have my understanding and ignorance judged, because we simply don't know what we don't know. So rather than have that be a stumbling block, I utilize it as a point of connection with the Trinity. Then it's more about my journey and adventure with my Father, Jesus and Holy Spirit as I come out from under the influence of the kingdoms of this world and into His kingdom. Relationship demystifies the process. As Proverbs 4:7 says, there is a way that seems right to a man, and in the end, it leads to death.

I have found that I get judged to the level of my understanding on any given issue and revelation continues to expand. Therefore, judging my understanding allows understanding to continue to expand as well.

The exchange is that we have our own and our ancestors sin and trading judged - and reposition under the truth that our Father meets ALL our needs according to His riches in glory. This is Deuteronomy 28, blessings and curses, choosing this day who we will serve. This is

Hosea, regarding the prostitute that was running after other lovers, this is our Father speaking tenderly to us in the desert, wooing us, telling us of His love and that the gifts (provision) are from Him but we didn't know. This is Israel in Egypt as slaves being brought out to inherit the promised land, this is manna in the desert, this is Jeremiah 29 past verse 11, where we seek him and find Him and he leads us out of captivity, this IS our redemption. This is the Isaiah highway of holiness, where only the redeemed walk and no beast can get up on it to devour, this is where we build up the road, pass through the gates and remove the obstacles from the way of my people! Ok, wow. Now after saying all of that, I am so full! I am really excited to see this at a depth I haven't before. Simplicity is the way to identify revelation from our Father.

Function:

*Father has provided His judgement for us to be sanctified.
*Jesus provided His blood to cover our sin under judgement.
*Holy Spirit provides indwelling guidance and comfort as we are being sanctified.

Pattern:

HIM-Jesus took all of our sin and shame, was accused, judged, found guilty, and killed. Then he asked us to pick up our cross and follow Him.

US-We follow him through the torn veil, take our sin and shame, are accused, found guilty, judged (under His Blood) as innocent, and CHOOSE to die to ourselves anyway.
It is simple in the basic scriptural concepts.

I had a similar frustration and angst as I hear from others, that initially led me into heaven. I was realizing that I had stewarded every revelation to the best of my ability, yet was left without my own personal needs for freedom and blessing being met in tangible ways. I say this because of years of being involved in healing ministry, deliverance, and inner healing, I have seen our Father do many beautiful things in the lives of others, many miracles. So, my suggestion to anyone feeling frustrated and lacking breakthrough is to go to Jesus and ask Him. Like face to face. He will begin to unravel what is holding you back - because something is. Set your desire to see him and let him teach you.

At first, I was a bit like a whiney, petulant child about these issues without resolve and He is so faithful. I found that what I had suffered under for years began to fall away, it truly is Him that leads us out of captivity! We have to see we are exiled captives though, which I am certain we all are seeing in some measure with some issues, and we are willing to acknowledge our need for Him in a greater way. One thing to note is that any mother and father become one and create a whole new bloodline in their children by the combination of their DNA. As we agree as one to create this bloodline, we can also repent and have any iniquity judged under the blood, even if we are divorced. Basically, either parent can deal with the iniquity of both bloodlines - because they became one, and reproduced that record of iniquity in their children. It requires taking responsibility for it all and functioning as a priest on behalf of your bloodline. The key to authority is love, as it covers a multitude of sin. And when we see how Jesus is our advocate as a high priest and our substitute, we recognize that we can take responsibility for sin as he took responsibility for all of it. We only do this being one with Him.

Everything I have judged in mobile court I do on behalf of my husband and I as 'one' being, our ancestors, and the bloodline we created together in our children. I function as a priest on behalf of our bloodlines.

Any conspiracy theory is an accusation being brought into the light. You can generally always function as a priest if you are willing to answer the accusations on behalf of the accused. This is part of the process and many times we *only* have a part to do. Example, abortion is part of trafficking as the parts are sold. This isn't theory. Yet, we are effective when we deal with our own house first.

You can go in and repent for your bloodline for the guilt of all these heinous sins. There are five positions to sin and repent from:

-Perpetrator
-Victim
-Condoner (in agreement with)
-Condemner (in self-righteous judgement of)
-Fearful (believing this is too powerful)

Receive His judgement under the blood of Jesus. Then, you can repent on behalf of the accused by taking responsibility for the sin and receiving His judgement under the blood. That is the foundation for any further legislative acts, that may or may not be your mandate.

I have found the way we learn is by doing, if we humble ourselves and always deal with our own house first, our Father is happy to show us His house. We have a tendency (based on our understanding of learning), to want to read or have it layed out for us prior to the 'doing' of anything. Starting is key and with almost certainty I can say it will be different than anything you thought you understand. We are being taught as we go, so there is always more.

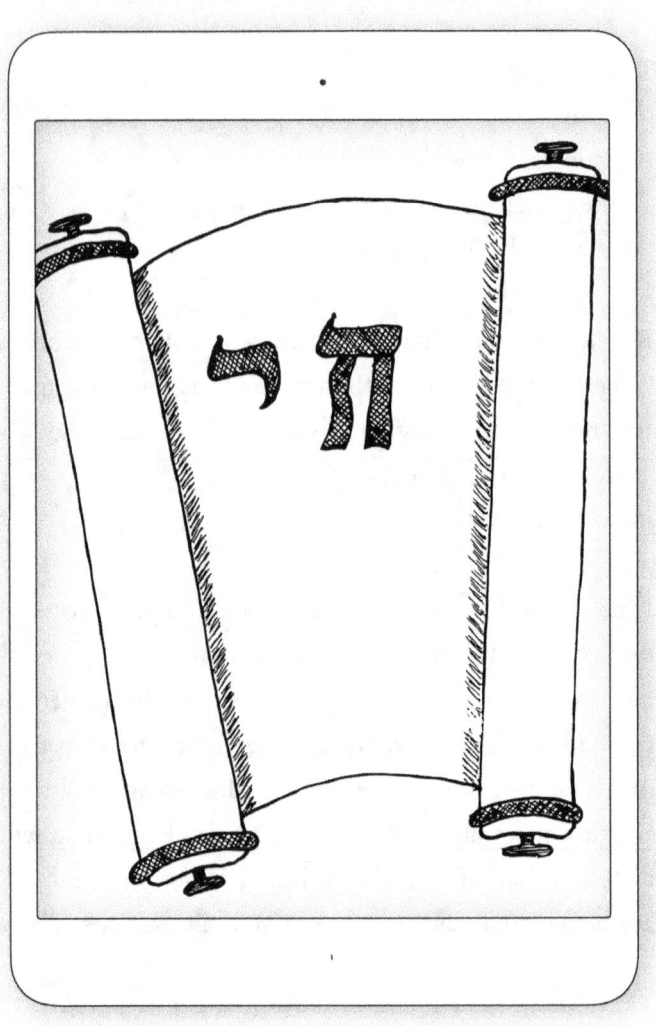

CHAPTER FIVE
Witness Stand - Seen and Unseen Testimony

This desire for justice and recompense or at least our version of it, is often (more than we recognize) rooted in a victim mindset and belief system. Victim thinking operates on a platform basis of pity, self-pity, entitlement and a righteousness of self. When we approach the mobile court from this place, we do not see results we are looking for. I have found that the more I have this position/mindset/belief judged in me, the cleaner my petitions are. The more I operate out of love, eliminating my debts to any man. And it all scales up, from my life to regional, geographic, to class action, to mankind, to all of creation. Romans 13:8 Let no debt remain outstanding, except the continuing debt to love one another, for whoever loves others has fulfilled the law.

Many would consider a victim as innocent either as an intended target of harm, or collateral damage in a circumstance. Whenever I am looking to 'see' how a victim sins, it generally includes having no voice and no choice. Giving up our voice and choice, false comforts like self-pity, resentment, vengeance, fantasy vindication, anything to cover shame such as addictions, gossip, slander, avoiding responsibility, blame, self-righteousness, unforgiveness, excusing or minimizing sin, permitting ourselves to be overmastered or deceived, silence, not exercising our choice, false humility that is actually pride, manipulative pride are all indicators of a victim position. These are all present in the overmastering of a victim.

There is a victim position for every sin, every trading floor, every oppression you can think of. Sometimes when I see a prevalence in an area like a victim mindset, I see how it's a grid I interpret every experience through. In that case I go get judged for responding to life and God as a victim, not just a specific sin.

Matthew 5:21-28 "You have heard that it was said to those of old, 'You shall not murder; and whoever murders will be liable to judgment.' 22 But I say to you that everyone who is angry with his brother will be liable to judgment; whoever insults his brother will be liable to the council; and whoever says, 'You fool!' will be liable to the hell of fire. 23 So if you are offering your gift at the altar and there remember that your brother has something against you, 24 leave your gift there before the altar and go. First be reconciled to your brother, and then come and offer your gift. 25 Come to terms quickly with your accuser while you are going with him to court, lest your accuser hand you over to the judge, and the judge to the guard, and you be put in prison. 26 Truly, I say to you, you will never get out until you have paid the last penny. 27 "You have heard that it was said, 'You shall not commit adultery.' 28 But I say to you that everyone who looks at a woman with lustful intent has already committed adultery with her in his heart.

When we bring our bloodlines into court for judgement, we are not only the accused but we also are a witness. Based on an example suggested of a bloodline that has an issue of the women submitting to controlling men identified, the ability to identify the issue is your witness of it. You see it, know it, experience it and can testify that your family functions this way. First you can go to court of accusation and take responsibility for the sin on behalf of the women in your family. Plead guilty to being controlling and manipulative, for trading with Jezebel for rulership authority and power, for rebellion against control, for being afraid of being controlled or controlling, for submitting to the oversight of controlling men, for not taking the rightful place in a marriage or within the body of Christ as co-labourers and co-heirs.

Then plead guilty on behalf of men for 'overseeing' the women, for acquiescing to control, rebellion against control, fear of being controlled or being controlling, for abandoning their wives, for not seeking His design of marriage, for not honouring their wives, for men pastors who teach and counsel contrary to God's design and truth. Everyone is participating in this dynamic and no single position is the 'righteous' one. Then ask that this whole package of Jezebel and Ahab rulership, hierarchy, ungodly power positions and rebellion in marriage, condemnation, condoning, and fear - be judged in the record of iniquity in your DNA, in your thoughts and intents of your hearts, and in any structures you have created by your agreement that are in operation in and around your life, all under the blood of Jesus.

Ask to be completely severed from the Jezebel/Ahab trading floor, from any misogyny rulership and false coverings. Then reposition yourself and your family as submitted under the headship of Jesus only, that He would govern your lives and marriages as the WAY, the TRUTH, and the LIFE. Love covers a multitude of sin, love provided our blood covering, love is our overseer.

Then ask Holy Spirit where other repentance to people may be needed. I've noticed things tend to unravel once we take responsibility for the sin, so generally you can expect a few more pieces to 'drop in' clearly. It is almost like focusing a lens on a camera, you see the main subject clearly, then as more focus and clarity comes, you see the fine details. When we can laugh at the absurdity of what was permitted in our blindness, this is the beginning of learning righteous judging. He who sits in the heavens laughs! So, we can too.

We also have the witness of a triggered response. Trigger warning - if a Facebook post (or anything you read, see or hear) has triggered a response in you that you recognize (primarily fear, anger and/or denial), sometimes accompanied by increased heart rate, change in rhythm of breathing, tingling, anger, urge to respond, sensation in chest or other physical symptoms, then this is the perfect time to address it, while the window is open.

Take a moment now to step into court and have the trigger judged under the blood. We can do this whether we know what it is connected to or not. I ask for the trigger to be judged, my response to be judged, my neural pathways to be judged, the brain chemical release I am experiencing to be judged, and then whatever record in my DNA that just got 'pinged', to be judged under the blood of Jesus. Then I ask to have the connections severed and I reposition myself under the government of my Father, Jesus and Holy Spirit.

This should cause a fairly immediate shift that is noticeable. I do this as a part of self-care and also my desire to not be ruled by something triggering me, but to live in peace and His rest. Then I pursue *with the Lord* what that was about and start having the sin judged, as it gets revealed to me.

Sometimes fear will try and hinder us from going to get our house judged, but you can take that in too for judgement under the blood.

If you are triggered by trigger warnings, use that to identify what our Father is trying to reveal to you personally. As we are all growing and maturing, our self-responsibility is a huge factor in how quickly we progress. It took me quite a while before I could go into court while in the midst of triggering. I often wanted to be right or mad or whatever my reaction was. The more I judged my own house, the more the judging timeframe tightened up. Rather than stew on something for a week, or go tell people about what happened to get my position validated etc., I would take it to my Father. Then it was only days before I could see my own response as sinful. Then it was hours, and now I can go in 'live' in the middle of a triggered response because I recognize it. I know what it feels like in my body and I know I want it exposed. I know I want to respond in LOVE all the time and that I still don't.

So, when we take these things to our Father, He is so happy because our heart matters to Him, our relationship matters to Him, our wellbeing matters to Him. A willingness to be accountable for our own junk is a massive key to maturing and progressing to look like our Father. We continually have everything that doesn't look like Him, judged and cleansed and transformed by the blood.

Someone had mentioned that being triggered is not a concept supported by scripture, to which I add that it is a concept supported by human experience. But yes, there are many scriptures to support self-control, being angry but not sinning, being wise, and patient, and kind, and gentle, guarding your heart for it is the wellspring of life, blessing and cursing from the same tongue, taking thoughts captive and subjecting them to the cross of Christ, search my heart oh Lord and see if there is any wicked way in me. I'm really talking about how we are partnering in our sanctification as a practical process. My question is why don't we have fruit when we need it or when we want to be fruit bearing in life?

The Word of God is also a witness. I consider that Jesus is the Word made flesh so therefore his very being is the word of his testimony. Likewise, we are the word of God, created in His image, at His word. So, we are the word of both His and our testimony.

I often use the basis of scripture about God creating mankind as part of my testimony. I AM CREATED IN THE IMAGE OF MY FATHER, and every other promise, description, truth, and plan of His for mankind also pertains to me as His creation. Generally speaking, I line up with The Truth of who I am. It's so powerful. It was a subtle shift in what I perceived to be a 'word of testimony', but a very powerful difference. And together with the Blood, the word of our testimony is how we overcome.

Sometimes the adversity we face, endure and overcome is what gives us a legal standing to gain a ruling in favour in His court and render reprieve and spoils. So much is needed for reprieve for our bodies like diabetes, cancer, mercury in our brain tissue, blood banks, transfusions and DNA infusions, DNA banks, seed banks (human and plant), energy trading, gender altering, child trafficking and the list goes on. The Israelites leaving Egypt with spoils is good example too, about leaving slavery with wealth. Shifting kingdoms and shifting kings. Jesus purchased us which means we have a previous owner, we weren't free-market beings.

Family lines join in marriage and create new family lines. Husband and wife become one, so we can function as a priest on behalf of both bloodlines, and the new bloodline we created if we have children. For others not in your bloodline, it is good to have a mandate, but there is much we can do without one. (Have the intent of your heart judged first to be clear on your motivation to act). Healing is the children's bread and we know it's His will to heal. His desire is that all come to salvation through Jesus. We can act on behalf of others' salvation. Jesus was wounded for our transgressions and love covers a multitude of sin. Expressions and actions that are done from love are always welcome and highly regarded. Sometimes I go to court of accusation to enter forgiveness on record for total strangers, because my heart is moved to do so.

We are witnesses to the truth of the corruption and iniquity in our bloodlines. It is like we have a DNA witness for or against us. My DNA record of iniquity will witness against me whether I think I have sinned or not. This isn't always the easiest thing to grasp because we like to have our own defense against accusations, rather than let the blood of Yeshua be our ONLY defense.

As we begin to see how our bloodlines witness against us regarding sin, we also begin to run to court knowing our only defense is the blood of Yeshua. We become willing to acknowledge the sin of the world rather than trying to 'be' righteous enough to avoid it. Our righteousness is as filthy rags, so as we 'see' this, we accept being clothed in his righteousness. This is such a beautiful exchange and an amazing real and legitimate (legislated) transformation.

We also have witnesses in this seen realm. We know who some of them are and sometimes those who provide witness against us are not known to us. If we look at gossip and slander or talking behind someone's back, this is a spoken witness against our character, words, actions or attitudes. It contains cursing against us as well. Sometimes we like to lump this into the 'false accusation' category of life and think it doesn't need addressing because it's not true or exaggerated, yet it still stands as a witness against us. Likewise, all the words we have spoken we are responsible for and will have to account for. This includes true and false, mean and malicious, unloving and unkind, condescending and arrogant and anything with any motive that wasn't love. This can seem daunting yet I have had the Holy Spirit show me this by category, by person, as threads throughout my life based on whatever I thought was 'okay' to say or felt justified in saying. Everywhere I provided a 'false witness' against someone or outright cursed them in my hurt or anger or need to be exalted. We have to give an account for every word so it is good to deal with this now and start running a 'live' version of having our words judged until we quit saying things like this. Somehow religious teaching has put this off into a judgement day scenario when we die. Or sometimes we look at unforgiveness and overlook everything we did, said and thought as a result of our unforgiveness.

CHAPTER SIX
Foreign Governments - Complicit Bloodlines

I have found five positions to sin from:
Perpetrator (doer of the deed)
Victim (intended target or collateral damage)
Condoner (in agreement with and complicit)
Condemner (in self-righteous judgement of)
Fearful (worry, anxiety, cautious, paralyzed or silenced)

The way the lord showed this to me was in regard to families in my bloodline. I'll use the sin of adultery as an example, in a scenario where a husband is cheating on his wife to identify this.
The husband is the perpetrator.
The other woman is perpetrator.
The wife is victim.
The children are the victims of the family breakdown.
The sister-in-law knows about it but doesn't want to get involved so is a condoner by silence.

The other woman's friend tells her she got a good catch so is a condoner by open verbal agreement.

The aunties gossip about the husband so are positioned as condemners being openly verbal about it.

The son knows of the affair and has building resentment towards his father and is a condemner in silence.

Everyone who knows there is an affair or suspects an affair, is afraid to say anything so they are fearful to bring it into the light or expose it therefore they are silenced or paralyzed.

The grown daughter begins to try and please her own husband in fear that he may have an affair too so she becomes anxious and cautious.

Then multiply that by generations and genders.

If I am going in to have adultery judged in my bloodline, I have to represent every position. I can also add trading into fear, deception, self-righteousness, self-pity, false refuges, everything anyone of this family would trade into as a result of adultery.

This is a priestly function of bringing in the collective sin of the people. It leaves no room to maintain an exalted position because 'we' don't sin like 'they' do. It also 'uncovers' the hidden ways we are still connected to the governance of the iniquity. It also clarifies for us that Jesus is our high priest who bore all of our sins and we are humbled to serve our bloodlines with Him.

I have been pondering Proverbs 6:16 in the context of trading with, and being ruled by Leviathan, king of the sons of pride.

This includes being a 'false witness'. When someone accuses us of something we did not do, and we defend our innocence, we become a false witness. Scripture says we will refute every tongue that accuses us but we don't refute with our innocence - we refute every accusation with the blood of Jesus. Because this is a framework of governance, we may be lied about or lied to and regardless, even as a victim we are complicit because there is obviously a sin record in our DNA that has Leviathan as our king rather than Jesus in whatever area.

It's like someone saying you are a manager working at xyz company, and you are only the assistant manager. So only part is true and part is false, yet you tell them that's not true. It may seem like splitting hairs yet it is imperative that we see our guilt and stop defending ourselves. Jesus' blood is our only defense, from the sin of all humanity.

If my bloodline committed a sin, and I didn't, when I am accused my inclination is to deny it. I am then a false witness. I am denying a sin that I am carrying a judgement against me and my bloodline for. So, my perspective is about going non-linear in terms of who sinned when. It's about the accusation of the sin and the record of the sin and the accompanying judgement against my bloodline that I carry in my DNA.

This was one of the issues that was part of my first initiation to the court by Jesus. I had the same accusation in almost the exact same words come at me, twenty years apart by two different people. I wasn't guilty of doing what I was accused of. I denied it both times.

Then I asked Jesus about it and we went to court and it was the most painful confession. Literal sharp stabbing pain in my chest and sobbing uncontrollably. What was happening is that there was a judgement of guilt against my bloodline that I was now having an opportunity to clear up. It was affecting my life even though I didn't do what I was being accused of.

Therefore, every time I denied this claim or accusation, I was a being false witness, because it was true, just not directly in my life. I had heard of generational blessings and curses but not generational judgements. This was learning how to 'function as a priest 101' for me and honestly after I was done in court with Jesus, this judgement that had been holding me back, was gone. If you asked me if I felt I was held back in that area, I would have said no because I honestly did not think I was.

I perpetuated this false witness as a reaction, being governed by Leviathan. In applying this to the human record of sin, not even just my bloodline, it eradicates the old man. We are a new creation. The key is being able to see it in order to apply it. Then I have wondered more generally why we would defend any accusation with anything other than the blood. In my case what I thought was truth was only partially true. It's a simple exchange of guilt for innocence that the blood of Jesus offers, and was offered, while we were yet sinners.

Then also a false witness in context of this scripture is not offering a true witness. Lying about events or people. Pouring out lies in some translations. It applies to an eyewitness or personal account. It is when I decide to cover someone with my words or explanation for any reason, even if it is a seemingly noble thing to do. Often, we will discount facts by understanding intentions. An example of this is thinking or saying "well, yes they said some mean things but they were hurting at the time", causing us to confuse judgement with mercy, and provide a minimized or downplayed and justified version of the truth, a false witness.

Haughty eyes, a proud look, pride, condescension, arrogance, thinking more highly of oneself than you ought, self-elevation and self-exaltation, egotistical, putting others down, viewing others as 'less than', pity and vanity.

This is the first thing in this scripture that the Lord hates, haughty eyes. It's about pride. The point is to recognize the government of Leviathan and how we trade into it and are subject to it.

A lying tongue - speaking lies, deceiving, intentionally luring someone into deception, false covering with words. Lies of omission in areas where we know full disclosure is required yet we withhold crucial or key information.

Hands that shed innocent blood - equals murder. This follows the escalation of offence, resentment, anger, bitterness, hatred, revenge, murder. The same as if you lust after someone you have already committed adultery, it is the same with anger, resentment, bitterness being equivalent to murder.

A heart that devises wicked schemes - plans for one's own gain at the expense of someone else, one who delights in wickedness, or delights in others being exposed, or the downfall of others. Schemes are strategies for evil.

Feet that are swift to run to evil - this is the action of the heart and the thoughts, when we act on it and participate in evil.

He who sows discord among his brethren - gossip, slander, accusation, defamation, libel, creating division, causing contention or fueling any of these with agreement.

We are reminded in Isaiah that we will refute every tongue that accuses us, that this is our vindication from the Lord, so a false witness or a true witness - all are covered by the blood.

Specifically, in Isaiah 54:17 it says our vindication is from the Lord, it is our inheritance to refute every tongue that accuses us. We refute by the blood. It is not only our inheritance but also the means of inheriting.

Proverbs 6:16 These six things the Lord hates, indeed, seven are an abomination to Him:
17 A proud look [the spirit that makes one overestimate himself and underestimate others], a lying tongue, and hands that shed innocent blood,
18 A heart that manufactures wicked thoughts and plans, feet that are swift in running to evil,
19 A false witness who breathes out lies [even under oath], and he who sows discord among his brethren.
Proverbs 6:16 AMPC

This is a pretty awful list of things the Lord hates and they are indicators of being a son of pride and serving king Leviathan, aligning with Satan, in direct opposition to our Father and His kingdom. This scripture becomes a way to identify a categorically complicit bloodline.

Other ways to identify areas of compliance to a foreign government is to recognize arcing which is a product of agreement. The following is from a post about recognizing when we arc, why we arc and the purpose and function of an arc.

Arcing is two in agreement and it opens a window into another realm and provides access for that government into the lives and situations of those involved. Which window opens depends on what government you are agreeing with, or trading with, or ruled and governed by. The record of iniquity in our DNA is what identifies what governments we are 'under'. These are often easily identifiable by our personal sin. It is harder to discern the things we don't do, or don't think we agree with, yet are still governed by. Our DNA with the record of our Father, identifies areas under His government.

Negative example:

I hate sin (any issue), completely disagree with sin (any issue), yet specific sins (any issue) have ruled as a government over my bloodline. I then 'arc' every time I encounter something in conversation regarding that sin because of the government over that specific sin issue and I continue to propagate this to my descendants, all the while thinking I am 'free' from that particular sin (any issue). When I go to have my bloodline judged, as a priest, I *have* to stand in all positions regarding sin.

Perpetrator
Victim
Condoner
Condemner
Fearful

I plead guilty to everything, have it all judged in my DNA, have all structures dismantled around my life and sever ties. Then I reposition my being, life and bloodline under the government of my Father; justice judgement holiness, Jesus; the way, the truth and the life, and Holy Spirit; righteousness, joy and peace.

Then, I read an article about a sinful scenario and nothing triggers inside me, or I hear a friend share about someone I know in a sinful scenario and nothing triggers in me. I am then able to act on behalf of someone without arcing. I'm not condemning, condoning, fearful, victim or perpetrator. I have been judged under the blood and the hooks are gone. I am not 'arcing' with control (opening up a Jezebel trading platform) because a sin (any issue) is intolerable, or heart breaking, or ungodly, or in pseudo-righteousness, or to feel important, or because I'm afraid or I'm driven by an unseen motive (like false justice) to DO SOMETHING about it. I am not driven or compelled or 'reacting'.

I can respond from a place of peace and I can check in and find out my part, if any. Chiefly, I am free to love in this area.

Positive example:

I love heaven, everything and everyone I have encountered in every realm. When I am in conversation with others about heavenly realms, it triggers in me and I agree and arc. This opens a window for the government of heaven to access my life and situations and of those involved in the conversation. Often angels show up, beings are attracted to the conversation, revelation abounds and wisdom flows.

We also arc wherever two are in agreement regarding anything, Matthew 18:19
"Again, truly I tell you that if two of you on earth agree about anything they ask for, it will be done for them by my Father in heaven".

Two people agreeing opens a window, three are a bench patterned by the Trinity, a fourth opens a door and we are a gate, so much more is going on in the spirit realm than we may perceive.

We are so much more powerful than we know! We arc all the time, so it is good to know what and who we trade with and what we are allowing access into the lives of those we are in relationship with.

Fishing Expedition example:

I am talking with a sports mom and she complains how her husband doesn't do any of the driving for her kid's sports activities. She suggests how she should take a weekend off and then he would 'have' to help with the driving!

She is in agreement with being a victim and is fishing for my agreement to dishonour her husband. She is also fishing for me to validate her use of manipulation and control. She is governed by and trading with Jezebel. If I agree (from any of the five positions), I will arc with her and the conversation will be taken over, leaving us both slimed. This will also be reinforcing that Jezebel trading floor as the governing structure over our relationship. Reinforcing Jezebel as ruler of both our marriages. We will feel used (as we actually were) and likely not know why. Even if I do know why in some measure, my resolve would have been either to not complain about husbands, or not talk to her as a way to get out from under the discomfort and slimy feeling.

If I don't agree, it dies on the spot because I am not arcing and not trading. Then I have no debt to any man except the debt to love and find myself able to love this woman.

Judgement is a provision from our Father, to sever ties, eliminate ungodly trading, close wrong realm windows, untether, untangle and come out and be separate and be purified. To be in the world but not of it. In His kingdom, submitted to and one with Him and His King and His Spirit.

To deconstruct and evaluate this example, the sports mom was acquiescing her choice. She positioned herself as a victim to her husband's choice to not drive the kids to sports and the obligation of her child to be in sports. She is engaging pride to comfort her so she can feel exalted above husband and child for her sacrificial service.

She is also afraid. Afraid to expect her husband to share responsibility, afraid to ask her husband to help with driving, afraid of confrontation, afraid he won't, afraid she won't know how to handle or resolve conflict and therefore she is willing to trade with Jezebel to get what she wants. Manipulation can solve this for her so he'll 'have' to drive and this meets her need to share the work load. She is willing to trade with Jezebel with others (other sports mom) to feel powerful again to meet need of feeling powerless. Also willing to trade with Leviathan (king over sons of pride) to feel ok about her lack of choice and inequality. This identifies some of her needs and how she is trading to have them met or fulfilled.

Things to judge in this example:
- Trading with Jezebel - manipulation, control and sense of gender power over other gender (unequal).

- Allowing other governance of 'choice' gate.
- Identity as victim - the tail not the head, beneath not above according to the Deut 28 curses for disobedience.
- Trading with Leviathan - being deceived, blindness, wishful thinking, fantasy, twisted communication and pride.

In this example, there isn't an innocent one, usually the perception of innocence is the victim - which is still arcing to permit the same governmental rulership. Our innocence comes from judgement under Christ's blood. Also, it is good to note here that no one 'is a Jezebel', they are governed by trading with Jezebel. It's a completely different understanding of spiritual governments, especially in a marriage where two are one.

We allow others to use us, we permit others to manipulate us, if she is fishing for freedom, it is from the wrong source, it's ok to judge her trading and not ok to condemn her for it. Part of a victim mindset or position is that you have no choice, no free will and it's a tough one to reconcile with truth, yet in self responsibility, it becomes more and more obvious.

I have found the more I get myself judged, the more I intuitively respond, so it's different with every fishing encounter. Sometimes I am acknowledging that the person agrees with something and feels that way. Sometimes I offer a balancing statement that indicates a self-responsible perspective on choice. Sometimes I just say, "oh", because I don't know what else to say or have anything to say, lol. The 'fishing' should end and I have noticed I can release love and compassion and mercy from my mountain while in conversation. This usually shifts the conversation because the 'other government' knows I won't engage with it, and love wins the airspace.

When we arc, it is opening a window to a government that we 'trade' with and into for supply of needs. This can be our Father's government and His riches in glory that supply all of our needs or it can be with some other ruler of this world. Sometimes recognizing the trading floor illuminates how we function with it and sometimes recognizing the arcing illuminates how we function with it. Both need to be recognized we need to consciously choose to come out of agreement.

For those who are wondering about functioning as a priest, there are many scriptures that explain this, we are a kingdom of priests. You take the sin as your own, in the function of a priest, as Jesus did for us, and we only do this in Him.

I would like to add, or maybe emphasize that the record of iniquity in our DNA that passes from generation to generation, if not judged, will remain. We are born under 'other' governance or, into slavery. This is very different from the idea or teaching that - I sinned and opened a door to a demon, or even familial spirits. The doors are in your DNA and they were opened before you got coded as a combination of your mother and your father's DNA. Those spirits are the agents to operate the earthly government, it's their job to look after those in their 'kingdom'. These are the kingdoms of this world.

In essence when we are judging ourselves by asking for and receiving our Father's judgement, under the blood covering of Jesus (so we don't die), are affecting the kingdoms of this world. The end game regarding this judgement is the transfer of rulership over us and all of creation.

So first we judge something in us, then as a priest for our bloodline, then we judge it around us, then we are able to, in love, act on behalf of others and judge (righteously), each time transferring rulership. The reason we are governed in the first place is because of trading. Ancestors and consequently us, trade with other entities for provision, to meet our needs, and we traffick whole bloodlines for our own gain.

We don't see we are doing this as clearly as say, an ancestor that gave their baby to the fire as a sacrifice to Moloch, but all those who have given up children for adoption, had them taken by child services, stillborn, infant death, missing, stolen, sold, trafficked, estranged, aborted etc. are all governed by the same god. This god and altar still requires a trade and a sacrifice as a debt you inherit, and are required to pay, legally. Jesus is our all sufficient sacrifice. So, when we recognize that there is pressure to sacrifice something, we can refuse and accept the substitution of Jesus as our all sufficient sacrifice on our behalf.

Religion - False Christianty

There is a level of living in a false Christian reality that we all need to address in our lives. If what we believe is creating our reality, then we must question it WITH the Lord. We need to have our minds renewed and submit our ways to His ways. This is not about the devil, it's about our inheritance as Sons of God. Part of cracking this open and exposing it, is the realization that all religion in the world is under an earthly government, including Christianity as we have known it. The dividing lines we draw to feel okay about the version of Christianity we are participating in, are by nature from the earthly religious government. A house divided against itself will not stand. This is a tough thing to sort through as there is so much good we want to hold on to. But if we recognize we are trying to discern the 'good' side of the Tree of the knowledge of good and evil, it becomes easier to scrutinize all of it. The difference we are identifying is not between good and evil, it is between good and LIFE.

Many believe that a Christian can't have a demon inhabiting their body or soul because we also have the Holy Spirit in us. Many find their belief system failing the reality of their life experience. Healing is another area where there are many misconceptions, as well as iniquity of the fathers being passed on to the children.

Untangling from a religious framework of powerlessness and ineffectual prayer does require relationship with our Father, Jesus and Holy Spirit. Where we simply just go and see them and talk to them and ask what needs to be different or what we need to see and know. The results are amazing as there is no more striving or guesswork when we enter His rest and cease from our own striving.

Religion will keep us striving and seeking for the 'right' combination of truths. Those in ministry for any length of time can tell you of the things that didn't turn out like they expected or of the people they couldn't help because they didn't know how.

I don't think the stronghold or earthly mountain of false religion is limited to Buddhism, Hinduism, Islam, Mormonism etc., I think it governs all religions and most deceptively the Christian religion. We have to parse the truth, to know it and Jesus is the TRUTH. Even what we believe can be filtered through mindsets that are strongholds. The only way I have found out of this tangled mess - is Jesus, in relationship, maturing and teaching me. Taking every thought captive and making it obedient to the cross of Christ includes the thoughts I have from teachings I have heard, or my perception of history basically everything I think and believe.

Even those who said Lord, Lord, did we not do these awesome things in your name, were told - depart from me, I knew you not. (my paraphrase). People are in pain, torment, lack, loss, suffering, slavery and bondage and don't know how to get out. All we (Christians) have to do is look at Deuteronomy 28 curses to recognize we are not living in His full provision for obedience.

If the deliverance movement, the prayer movement and the inner healing movement had produced the full results we seek, we would not continue seeking. Though He is not far from us as we are told in Acts 17:26. My way of escape is His judgment, His blood covering and His counsel. I love it. I had no idea we could just go to His house in heavenly realms. To His court and His government, to actually function in that seat at the right hand of our Father, with Christ. We need to keep ascending because there is no end to the increase of his government.

As a government in regard to Freemasonry, ignorance or blindness is a tactical vow and part of the cursing. It is how it remains 'occulted', 'secret' or 'hidden'.

Freemasons traffic their descendants before they are born and everything remains in 'active status' until someone in the bloodline deals with it. As an example, I had nine car accidents in eighteen years of driving until getting free from Freemason curses. Then I had zero accidents in the next twenty years of driving.

Everything you do in court regarding freemasonry is also for your descendants that aren't born yet. You are taking back your bloodline, whether your family sees this or not, you are removing the agreement with blindness.

It can freak people out when they begin to see the governmental power structure of freemasonry in high level positions in every arena of global life. Jesus' governmental power structure is more important to see, as the kingdoms of this world become the kingdoms of our God and of His Christ. Mountains will overtake mountains and so even though it can be freaky to watch unfolding, it is a source of great joy in that He already overcame the world.

Regarding 'cleansing bloodlines', it is tough with terminology because the statement means so many things to so many people. If we are doing the same thing and not seeing change, then there is more to it. I consider that pursuit to be for more understanding. When we get ourselves and our bloodlines judged, it is really only to the level of our understanding. For example, I took ten minutes and read directly off of a document to get judged for ungodly trading on ungodly trading floors. I went in with the understanding that someone in my bloodline somewhere has committed every possible sin, trading with other gods for power and provision. My thinking changed overnight. I did it again with some friends a couple of days later and there was so much more that I couldn't see or understand the first time that I could then also have judged. So, it became obvious that the more I got judged, the more I could see. I revisited trading floors as I gained a deeper understanding of what is traded, why it's traded and with whom, and that I am a trading platform as well.

I consider this the spiral of revelation. It's not just going around the issue one more time, or something (enemy) not complying with a court judgement, but a deeper revealing of the same thing. We learn from Jesus how to govern or rule in Him, our own life from our mountain, a little more each time. In hindsight, I am always thankful for the delicate way he has brought me into an understanding. And I am not regretful at all about the time it took me to get there. If you still have regret about what you didn't know, keep pursuing that area of exposé with Jesus until you have no regret.

This spiral of revelation is a delight, always in motion, untethering us from this world and its cares. You will know the truth and the truth will set you free. It is a deepening relationship with Father, Son and Holy Spirit, a deeper revealing of them to me, and increasing love, peace and rest. Learning how to govern - to be above and not beneath, the head and not the tail, and the rest of the Deuteronomy 28 blessings for choosing who I serve.

Regarding another person repenting themselves for their own sin, yes, they need to get there on their own. In the meantime, LOVE covers a multitude of sin and the priestly function is one of LOVE. Judgement is a provision from our Father, it is for our benefit, so to be available to access His judgement for another person is a loving, beautiful and helpful thing. They are covered by the blood, the judgement is for the government of other gods, trading and sin.

As for functioning in Christian witchcraft, when you first go in to have your 'emotional care' judged for whom you want to act on behalf of, what you come out with is a purified motive. We should owe no one any debt except LOVE. The heart is deceitful above all things, who can know it? We create with intent, so if we are governed by fear and control, but think we are well meaning, we will not see the rebellion as witchcraft in fear and control we are operating under and 'arcing' with for that person. We will end up fortifying a governmental structure over their (and our) life, thinking we have done an awesome thing. And this will be in some other court, or doesn't even have to be in court, can be from prayer too, with our words. There is a way that seems right to a man and in the end, it leads to death. Get all your ways that 'seem right to you' judged. Fear of the Lord is the beginning of wisdom and the result of seeking wisdom is to understand the fear of the Lord.

If we bump up a level of government and look at the ungodly governance of children categorically, we see Moloch, Baal, Baphomet etc. This covers the ungodly governing hierarchy of stealing, killing and destroying of children as the 'family court system', 'government child welfare', 'orphanages', 'abortion industry and practice', 'adoption agencies', 'child pornography', 'child soldiers', 'child sex trafficking', 'NGOs for missing children', 'rape a virgin aids cure in Africa', 'young blood elixirs', 'child workers', and 'child brides'.

This is OUR sin, we have done this to children for thousands of years, this is what we repent for (and our ancestors), for child sacrifice, murdering children and trafficking children - TRADING AND SACRIFICING CHILDREN AND BLOODLINE DESCENDANTS FOR OUR OWN GAIN.

Then we ask for judgement under the blood of Jesus for being a perpetrator, victim, condoner, condemner, fearful- for being complicit in that which we hate.

Leviticus 26:40-42 "'But if they will confess their sins

and the sins of their ancestors—their unfaithfulness and their hostility toward me, which made me hostile toward them so that I sent them into the land of their enemies— then when their uncircumcised hearts are humbled and they pay for their sin, I will remember my covenant with Jacob and my covenant with Isaac and my covenant with Abraham, and I will remember the land.

To clarify what I mean by NGOs for missing children, I mean a non-government organization (business, charity or foundation) acting as a missing child cataloguing service (Child Find), a child rescue organization, or providing orphanages in a disaster situation (like Haiti), that are running child trafficking operations and need untraceable access to children. These are cover organizations.

In a priestly function, we take the collective sin before the Lord and take responsibility for it. Judgement is a pronouncement of guilt, it is a provision from our Father to separate us from iniquity and sin. The blood of Jesus is provision to withstand His judgement, as He has paid our penalty by shedding it into the earth and it becomes a witness to our redemption. We then can receive His forgiveness. Forgiveness is a provision only for the guilty. I believe this is the 'technical aspect' of sanctification.

In this case, Father - judge us for we have sinned against children in all these areas. The 'other' government is judged as well, without the provision of the blood of Jesus, in this case it is the Moloch hierarchy and any other governing structure over children.

You can also begin to take your household into court to receive judgement as it purifies. Categorically, go plead guilty on behalf of your bloodline including your descendants for (this scenario was for an underage daughter dating an older man):

- Rebellion, control, hardened heart, defiance,
- Child sacrifice, prostitution, unholy sex, illegal sex, fornication, lust, rape,
- Rejection, abandonment, condemnation, shame, abdicating responsibility,

This is a start from the example that was shared in the Facebook group and what follows is a quick process.

These are governments we trade with, and even if we are unable to identify the 'other god' this is connected to, you know it is not our Father's kingdom. The more I untether from these governments, the more I see a deeper level of entanglement. Plead guilty to have sin judged as:

Perpetrator, Victim, Condoner, Condemner, Fearful
(Any position can arc, open a window, allow governance)

1) Judge me and my bloodline under the blood of Jesus.
2) Judge everything in and around my life where this is in operation with the same judgement.

3) Sever any ties, untether my DNA and my being from connections to these governing entities and any altars they trade on.

4) I choose this day to reposition my life and being and my family under the government of my Father. To tether to the Kingdom of my Father; to justice, judgement and holiness. To tether to His King, Jesus who is the way, the truth and the life. And tether to His Spirit, who is righteousness, joy and peace. I align in submission to righteousness and justice as the foundations of His throne. This is done in the court of our Father or another term is the judicial and legislative functions of our Father's kingdom. This whole process is a legal process.

If we can see the structural components of realms and dimensions and how entangled we are in these governmental mountains, we can see why this isn't just a 'nice prayer to pray'. We are literally coming out and being separate, being in this world but not of it. A stranger or sojourner in the kingdoms of this world. All of humanity is now like a bowl of mixed DNA alef-bet soup, being recoded as beholding Him with an unveiled face.

1 Corinthians 3:18
And we all, with unveiled face, beholding the glory of the Lord, are being transformed into the same image from one degree of glory to another. For this comes from the Lord who is the Spirit.

CHAPTER SEVEN
Transfer of Rulership - Overcome the World

The idea of a petition for recompense or compensation should be *almost* irrelevant as we mature. As we grow in understanding of our function and participation within the kingdom of our Father, we should see clearer, we are the older brother who ALREADY HAS EVERYTHING. Likewise, in the story of Job, he didn't ask for double what he lost, his fortunes were restored by the Lord. There are many scriptures about the Lord restoring fortunes, often before their very eyes. Do a search, it is quite encouraging.

Job 42:10-11 After Job HAD PRAYED FOR HIS FRIENDS, the Lord restored his fortunes and gave him twice as much as he had before. All his brothers and sisters and everyone who had known him before came and ate with him in his house. They comforted and consoled him over all the trouble the Lord had brought on him, and each one gave him a piece of silver and a gold ring.

A quick internet search will show lists of scriptures related to the word recompense, it is for the wicked as well as the righteous. Many of us want to ask for recompense and yet we do not know what we are asking. If there is wickedness, you may reap that recompense. Because of this nature of recompense, I believe we can trust our Father to restore our fortunes. I also believe that we can talk to him about this and gain understanding. Often (like mentioned before), we approach court from a victim perspective looking for some measure of what we perceive as justice. What we can be certain of is that we receive forgiveness from our Father, as part of the exchange that Jesus paid for us.

I have pondered what this scripture means and how it would apply to court and legalities. John 20:23 If you forgive anyone's sins, their sins are forgiven; if you do not forgive them, they are not forgiven.". Mark 2 in context explains the transfer of authority to forgive sin on earth, which I find fascinating. Mark2:7 "Why does this fellow talk like that? He's blaspheming! Who can forgive sins but God alone?" 8 Immediately Jesus knew in his spirit that this was what they were thinking in their hearts, and he said to them, "Why are you thinking these things? 9 Which is easier: to say to this paralyzed man, 'Your sins are forgiven,' or to say, 'Get up, take your mat and walk'? 10 But I want you to know that the Son of Man has authority on earth to forgive sins." So, he said to the man, 11 "I tell you, get up, take your mat and go home." 12 He got up, took his mat and walked out in full view of them all. This amazed everyone and they praised God, saying, "We have never seen anything like this!" Jesus wanted us to know this even before his blood sacrifice was completed. I feel confident to engage the record in heaven to add my forgiveness for people. Sometimes it is a stranger, sometimes it is someone I know and I choose to forgive them on record. I desire more understanding of this specifically as it represents and incredible transfer of authority, from Jesus to us, wow.

Personal and group example:

This is an example of taking accusations in to have judged: One day I decided to post a vent of sorts in the Courtrooms of Heaven Facebook group. I should have recognized that any 'vent' is wrought with self-righteousness, but alas, my Father was teaching me something, publicly. I will share it here also as it was extremely beneficial to me.

I have noticed that when people are asking for help understanding courts, or help with a circumstance in their life and how to deal with that in court, often the comments are filled with prayer strategies, deliverance prayers, intercession ideas etc. As this is a Courtrooms of Heaven group, I'm wondering if we (individually and corporately) need to plead guilty to the sin of pride and rebellion. It is as if we are collectively complicit in 'doing it our own way', 'not humbling ourselves to learn from Jesus', 'trying to divert those who are seeking court help back to a prayer method' and 'still promoting a distant relationship and methods that require no relationship'. I love the collective experience and revelation of the body and think what this group has facilitated and fostered is awesome. If we keep the focus on Courtrooms of Heaven (responses, experience, testimonies, questions and answer) I believe we will accelerate collectively. I think this is an example of the difference between patching an old wineskin and putting new wine into a new wineskin. Rebelling against the new revelation in the pride of previous revelation which is subtle because we don't appear as Courts haters.

I will include my responses to the comments only because it helps explain where I am coming from in my understanding.

Maybe it's a semantics issue what people mean and understand by the words; prayer, intercession, warfare and deliverance yet I am speaking about people who are specifically seeking understanding about Courtrooms of Heaven.

You can pray and petition at the throne of Grace as well - it is a provision from our Father as well as judgement is. You can intercede with the one who makes intercession for us in learning how to function as a priest (dealing with sin, guilt, forgiveness). You can mandate Angels from Angel's court and have them do warfare on behalf of the saints, as a commander with authority and legal papers. You can legislate as a king, as we are kings and priests. Maybe the distinction is made clearer by saying, 'functioning in the Courts and Governmental system of Our Father, in Heaven'.

Well basically we are pursuing understanding to function in the Courts of Heaven in this group. The basic level is the Court of Accusation, where we are hindered by accusations against us and our bloodline. We ideally go to court to get ourselves judged under the blood of Jesus for our own sin, and also have the accusations judged. I am suggesting that together we are in pride and rebellion if we continue to act like we have all the answers outside of relationship with Jesus. Most of these 'answers' are not from engaging heaven, or court in heaven. Many are rote methods that do not require any intimacy with Jesus, or even much relationship or responsibility, nor accessing Heaven. So, if in a Courts of Heaven group, I continue to advise you to 'just pray' or 'leave it in God's hands' or 'bind the spirit of such and such' - I am rebelling against the purpose of the group. I can advise all those things in other groups but this one is related to Courts of Heaven. Also, on a grander scale, if there is a provision from our Father, in Heaven, that He is revealing (legal issues for Court in Heaven), and inviting us into and I tell you "don't access heaven, stay in this realm and let God sort your troubles, or go to war with some demons in this realm, or pray this prayer", I am then hindering you.

I think a reason I would do this is pride (exalting my own understanding) and rebellion (against God's understanding).

If this were a 'learn how to sculpt with limestone' group and every time you asked a question about how to sculpt, you were told to paint with acrylics instead of sculpting, wouldn't that seem odd to you? I think we should corporately learn together how to identify our sin for what it is and go get judged under the blood for it. And that we may accelerate our understanding, growth and maturity if we humble ourselves to learn about the Courts & Government of our Father, in Heaven.

I am not an admin of the group so I am not speaking on behalf of the group itself, this is my observation and I'm one of almost 15,000 members (at that time) and we are both powerful to have our thoughts on things, and I agree that no one has all the answers. I think we agree that more focus on Jesus is needed and it is Him who shows me my sin, so they kind of go hand in hand for me the deeper I go in relationship with the Trinity. If you don't feel this post applies to you, then please disregard it, it is meant for those who it does apply to, me included. If I understand what you are identifying (in relation to Courtrooms of Heaven) is that some are arrogant in their operation in courtrooms? If so, then yes, this is the pride-ditch on the other side of the road, and I agree we need to repent of elitism. All is wrong trading for self-exaltation. Leviathan is the king of the sons of pride. Our best approach is having our pride, arrogance, elitism, know it all, righteousness of our own, right-ness and condescension judged for the sin it is. And humble ourselves to learn from our head who is Jesus, how to operate in the Courtrooms of Heaven.

My viewing people through the eyes of love is to call us higher, out of the sin that so easily entangles us. If we can see our sin, it is easily dealt with. If we deny our sin, well, then we live like that. It is His kindness that leads us to repentance, and therefore it should also be my kindness that leads us to repentance. If we are in pride, then let's humble ourselves, if we are in rebellion, let's submit to our King, Jesus. Often our busy lives demand our attention and focus. At first, I would go to court while doing errands and driving in my car because it was 'alone time'. When you add up all the bits here and there, it was like a regular appointment with Jesus to teach me about the court of accusation and then other courts. He can work with whatever our situations are, and can infuse understanding to maximize our time.

I did notice that the more I dealt with trading floors in court, getting myself judged, my life slowed down, my busy thoughts slowed down and I had more peace. Even a simple start at migrating my life under the blood, I found fruitful right away.

Through the course of the very busy comment thread, I held my position, explained myself, explained in more detail, agreed and disagreed with some things being said, defended myself, answered other questions, and liked comments. What I wasn't prepared for was the volume of accusations that came at me. Some were veiled in generalities, some were specific and direct and they covered a variety of angles and positions of sin. Somewhere during the course of this morning, I messaged an admin of the group to confess my 'live' triggered posting and apologize. And that I would seek Wisdom on what to do in order to take responsibility for what I had just done, and the trigger-fest it opened up. I felt the course of action was to take responsibility for the accusation I had partnered with in my original post and every accusation that revealed itself in the comment thread. To model the very thing that I was accusing people of not doing. Insert foot in mouth here. I was laughing at myself and with my Father as He showed me very clearly my own pride and rebellion! Oh my, the grace He affords me is so sufficient. What follows is my public walk-through of getting myself judged for every accusation in its original wording that showed up in the comments plus a few Holy Spirit added for me.

COURT OF ACCUSATION

For my own benefit, I am going to address my pride and rebellion, and for the benefit of the group, I am going to address it here in this thread. I come before the court today to plead guilty to the sin of pride and rebellion, the accusations against me have come before me and the court. I plead guilty to the following as a perpetrator, a victim, a condoner (in agreement with), a condemner (in self-righteous judgement of) and in fear of. I am guilty of being harsh, uncaring, unloving, legalistic, I have no grace for learners, I am not willing to give a pass to unrelated comments, I am religious, I do not focus enough on Jesus, I focus too much on sin, I don't address other issues in the group that are important, I am not mature enough to just pray about things on my own without posting. I have judged the new people in this group, I have judged people in this group self-righteously, I am wrong about believing that suggestions other than Court are rebellion or pride, what I teach about Courts is not as loving or helpful as other Courts teachings, I think I have this figured out, I think I am God. I think I can know people's heart motives, I am over evaluating what is being done in this group, I don't have grace for where everyone is at on their journey, my focus is wrong, I am not viewing through the eyes of love, I think it is my place to lead people to repentance. I say prayer and intercession and deliverance is wrong, I say things that are not biblical, I say things that are in direct rebellion to scripture, I am high and mighty, I think I am exalted because of special revelation and knowledge of Court, I am part of a cult and teach like a cult, I have a religious spirit, I am in rebellion to God and to the bible. I am a hypocrite, I don't like being corrected, I resist those who point out my sin, I want to maintain my self-exalted position, I am not humble, I am not teachable, I not only think I am like God but I think I am better than God, I try to keep those wanting to access heaven away from heaven, I lie to keep people from receiving the provision of judgement and forgiveness from their Father. I intentionally block the gate people are trying to go through to access heaven, I have a lying spirit and I am a lying spirit, I have a religious spirit and I am a religious spirit. I have traded with traded with Athaliah, daughter of Jezebel for my identity, I have traded with Jezebel for my own way, I have traded with Leviathan as the King of the sons of pride for an exalted position of importance, I have traded with Apollyon in fear of sharing the gospel of truth and traded it for another gospel.

I ask to be judged for these sins of pride and rebellion, and my ungodly trading to get my needs met, under the blood of Jesus, I ask that you judge my bloodline, judge the record of iniquity in my DNA, judge every neural pathway that includes these sins, trading, mindsets and beliefs, judge the record in every cell in my body, under the blood of Jesus.

I also ask that you judge every governmental structure in operation in and around my life, that I have helped create with my agreement, judge them with the same judgement you judge me with. I ask that every connection and tie to the government of pride and rebellion, and to these ungodly trading floors be fully severed.

I ask that every area in me that triggers in response to serve pride and participate with it, serve other kings and kingdoms of this world would be cleansed by the blood of Jesus.

Today I choose to humble myself and submit my life and being and bloodline under the government of my Father, to His Kingdom, to justice, judgement & holiness. To His King, Jesus who is the way the truth and the life, and to His Spirit who is righteousness, joy and peace.

I ask for Court ordered enforcement of this judgement, for Angels to dismantle and untether and untangle my life, my being and my bloodline, from the fabric of the government of pride and rebellion, from these trading floors, that I may come out and be separate.

Father, I thank you for your provision of judgement to cleanse me, Jesus for your blood that I may withstand the judgement, and Holy Spirit for your ever-loving counsel and kindness that leads me to repentance. And to this group and its leadership, I ask you also to forgive me for the sin of pride and rebellion.

What followed afterward was an incredible freedom and humbling and I continued to see areas where I was in agreement with pride and religious pride in many other areas. I was very thankful this was brought into the light so I could see it and have it judged as it began to unravel many other things for me personally. Others that read through to the end of the comment thread where this was posted also benefitted from such a lovely thorough list of accusations, or at the very least, witnessing my Father humble me with such love. There is therefore no condemnation for those who are in Christ Jesus. What joy!

I have found that as a result of deepening my face to face relationship with Jesus, it is Him who shows me the very things some perceive are a distraction from Him when it comes to creation and heavenly realms. Some people refer to these as 'rabbit holes' with the evil intent of the Alice in Wonderland example. I think it is important to recognize when Jesus wants to reveal something in greater detail. Also, to note if we are 'lured' by the knowledge of good and evil. It is Him who wants us to see, know, understand, be wise as serpents and harmless as doves. Everything that stands in our way of what we are to govern, will be revealed by Him. The desire to know and understand can be motivated by fear or love, if fear then it needs to be purified. If love, then it becomes a victorious unfolding of His nature, His kingdom, our purpose, and great fun in relationship with Him and union with Him.

If I am in a corporate setting, I am usually on my mountain and I don't really get bothered by anyone. When we remove our grid of how the demonic operates, it allows us to come right out of agreement with anything troublesome or dangerous and not frame it. Like people in the same realm, but we are shifting our source of supply by shifting our gaze. It is powerful when I look at things from my mountain, and grow in rulership and governance of my sphere. There is far more to see and less wasted time, effort and distraction.

You can always go first to have your own house judged for participating with this spirit (Python) in any way such as ancestors trading with it and sacrificing to it. Receive judgement under the blood of Jesus, ask to be separated from any connection to it and reposition your bloodline under the government of our Father.

Then engage with Jesus or Wisdom as to how to proceed. First, if you have a mandate to act on something - and if so, ask what to do. Sometimes things are revealed to us because our Father is trying to teach us and show us something, not necessarily to 'act on it' today, although it could be. It a grand adventure to be taught by the Lord. Every time something is shown to me, I have my house judged. I am regularly reminded of the scripture - who may ascend the hill of the Lord? He who has clean hands and a pure heart.

I'm super big on having our own heart and bloodline judged. We tend to function on deep levels of 'accepted' fear, pride and control and these become way more obvious the deeper we go into 'looking and being' like our Father. I have been surprised at the depth of some justifications and mental gymnastics I wrap sin in, yet I am always grateful when it is uncovered and unraveled.

There seems to be a regular desire I hear from others to 'do' something in court in heaven for someone else like a family member, friend, or a people group. There are other options to act on behalf of someone else, we can go boldly before the throne of grace, or go to angel's court for existing scrolls. Have you been to Angel's court yet? There are many scrolls that have already been approved on behalf of creation, mankind, individuals, geographical areas, the cosmos. They are waiting for us to show up there and take responsibility for them. They are mandates and you can request them there. They could have been initiated by our Father, our ancestors, men in white linen, or the cloud of witnesses. You don't necessarily need to know how to initiate a scroll and have it approved in order to go there and see what is available and request it. Our motivation needs to be love though and judging our desire to 'help' others can purify hidden fear and desire to control.

I didn't read any books about Angel's court, I heard about it on a podcast and then I went with Jesus and He showed me things. I love those who are willing to share on podcasts and other teachings about their experiences in heavenly realms as it causes a desire in me to pursue more understanding from Jesus. I often feel like I am putting together a big puzzle and always looking for pieces I didn't see before.

Someone brought up the seven cultural mountains teaching and I had heard it said that this is about Nephilim ruled and other mountains, so we don't need to 'take' these mountains or even try or desire to. Then I questioned that with the Lord to show me what this actually means and looks like. I found out it's true. By this I mean they are governed by spirits that are not of God, they are Nephilim. They are in essence the 'kingdoms of this world'. If you engage them in the spirit, to have a look, you will see this. Our position as sons is to create different mountains altogether.

We create new mountains around responsibility and authority. That being said, we have our personal mountain or mountains to deal with. Some people see multiple mountains for their marriage, finances, health etc. and some rule all areas of their life from one mountain. Sometimes your mountains merge or stack and become one. I think this is based on revelation of different ways to govern, like a progressive revealing.

Jesus is Lord or Lords, so we have mountains we learn to function as a lord over.

He is also the king of kings and as we learn to function as a king, we see kingly mountains emerge or form and some of these are a responsibility for a greater sphere of influence. These all have thrones and crowns and coronation events. The structure becomes more obvious the more time you spend engaging rulership. Your personal mountain for your life has gates and a treasury as it follows a temple pattern. This is connected to court as well in the sense that you land everything through the gate that you are, including angels.

As an example of my choice gate, I went to mobile court to take responsibility for everything in my life having been and currently being, my choice. I plead guilty for anything I could think of relating to my choice in every area of my life. For example, areas and circumstances where I let others choose for me, or where I chose to please others, or abdicated my choice, or had a limited palette of choices due to blindness or victim perspective believing I had no choice. I plead guilty for bad choices, ineffective choices or not making choices (which is also choosing) in relationships, business, family, health, finances and any area I could think of. I asked to be divorced from anything affecting or ruling my choice gate, and then I went there to occupy the throne with Wisdom and Jesus.

It was an awesome experience. I now see choices I never saw before and I feel released to choose unhindered or without pressure. There are still issues in certain areas but I now have wisdom and righteousness involved in my choices. It was quick and produced dramatic, tangible, immediate results. It is also a position to go forward from, even if some choices are still difficult to see my way through, I am now being taught how to exercise my choice. Choosing is now something I am able to take responsibility for and if I am unable to see my options, I go find out why right away. Everything pertaining to my maturing is progressive it seems, and I am very delicately walked into deeper issues by Jesus in a very precise order and timing. For this I am thankful as I don't know what I don't know.

CHAPTER EIGHT
Going Forward

I have been having my house judged for several years now and can't say I am nearing an end. It really is about the journey and the deepening of relationship with our Father, Yeshua and Holy Spirit. I have seen remarkable growth and others in my life can testify as witnesses to the changes and growth. I would be remiss if I didn't mention the threshold guardians we encounter as we enter into our destiny, and remove the obstacles for the destiny of our bloodline. This is no small feat, and as one of the admins in the Courtrooms of Heaven Facebook group mentioned, it is not a process for sissies.

I will very emphatically recommend that you seek out Anne Hamilton's material on threshold guardians. She has written a number of books and has a lot of material on Facebook. I was led to her material when I needed to know what I was up against, what was required of me and how to deal with what seemed like an invisible enemy. Some of these threshold guardians are identified as entities we trade with yet what I began to see was repeating patterns that would only progress so far and then fade away. This had me chasing the ever elusive breakthrough. There is such precision in scripture and the language of our Father. Every word and action recorded of Yeshua in his time on earth was so intentionally redemptive. Scripture is a code and even with our human changes to it over the years, and our often very wrong teachings, our Father is well able to reveal himself through this code and bring order into the unseen.

I have found that I need a balance of seeing what I am up against, what is being asked or demanded of me, what Yeshua has done for me and what I am actually supposed to do. So recognizing how my enemy operates is good to know but not to focus on. This isn't spiritual warfare, it is spiritual growth into our authority as sons. We need to be above the kingdoms of this world. We overcome by the blood of the lamb and the word of our testimony which is our destiny. We overcome with the fruit of the spirit, it's kind of like a mandatory growing up in all things before we cross into greater responsibility. I believe this is also a protection from our Father, again, because we don't know what we don't know.

We need to see the depth of every area we are asked to do for ourselves that which Yeshua already did for us. He is our all sufficient sacrifice, we don't need to sacrifice ourselves or others to step into destiny. We don't need to trade with any other entity because our Father meets all our needs according to His riches in Glory. Yeshua tore the veil and provided access for us. Our Father and His name are our only refuge in times of trouble. We don't need any other false refuge to run to. He is a shield about us so we do not need to have our own shield. He is our glory so we do not need any other glory from anyone or anywhere. He is the lifter of our head, our government. We do not need to trade with any other entity to leverage our authority.

So hopefully you can see how crossing a threshold into destiny requires us to shed every other method we thought we should employ, any tactics we have used in the past (for generations actually), or any other self -directed idea. It requires us reflecting the image we are created in, and love, as everything is fulfilled in love. We come out from every other ruling entity's governance, out from our self-governance and into a new way, new man, new life, new beginning.

This does not mean you are not doing what you are supposed to be doing in the sense of 'activity' or 'purpose' in this life. You may make changes as you see things clearer, you may not, but the being that you are will change.

As for the destiny of your bloodline, you may not see how this will affect things in future generations. I only catch glimpses now and again, but there is a deep drive for righteousness in me. It is for freedom that Christ has set us free, the ultimate breakthrough.

The bigger the picture gets for me, the larger the purpose within it is. There is a progression for our destiny and we are always progressing in it. We are eternal beings and all is purposeful. Whether we can see why or how we are releasing the destiny of our bloodline, we are. We in fact are being for our bloodline what Jesus is for us as individuals, a high priest. He who has been forgiven much, loves much.

It really is a journey, this life. It's a journey as a new creation in Christ. We have been genetically modified from our original image and we are recognizing that in a way that religion has clouded us from seeing. I am so thankful for those who have pioneered beyond the veil on behalf of mankind. I believe they have removed obstacles on the highway of holiness, and built up the roads, passed through the gates as described in Isaiah. The best and only thing I can do is agree with our Father. That requires seeing where I haven't been in agreement with Him which is often painful to recognize, but so delightful to know that His judgment leads to triumphant mercy.

I wish I had more to offer in any way to explain the beauty of His holiness. I am sure I am only scratching the surface yet I thought it beneficial to some if I compiled my words, thoughts and limited understanding. I am often amazed when I read my own words, wondering how I could know these things yet am reminded of His mercies that are new every morning and His grace that is sufficient. Every day is new, I have heard it said that there is an angel who reads our scroll every morning. I haven't experienced this but knowing someone else has causes me to desire to know my part in His story. There is a contentment in knowing that all is as it should be for today. Even if my circumstances or slow growth seem to hinder anything in my life, the joy set before me encourages me onward.

My hope is that you are encouraged in some way by having read this and that you have an increased view of the amazing provision of our Father's judgment, Yeshua's blood and the counsel of the Holy Spirit. If you have been a part of the Courtrooms of Heaven Facebook group for a while, you have likely read much of these words as I have been growing up in the group. I consider it an honour to be part of the online heavenly realms community. I find our Father's strategic connections to be quite amazing. I would have never expected to be finishing a fourth book regarding destiny. Participating in the online community has been a very interesting way to write books without intending to and I am thankful for every comment, question and answer. I do have one more book to write for this destiny scroll series and it will be about ruling and will be purple. I will confess, I did not realize these books were on my scroll until they just started 'happening' yet I am so delighted.

The way I was shown there was a fourth book was by using an online colour palette generator. I had the first three colours in the palette and this colour kept populating the fourth position. Finally it struck me that it was supposed to be the cover colour for the fourth book. I laugh because it is so simple yet so fun walking through this with our Father. The children's series I am writing under a pen name I have known about for a long time and was waiting for certain timing. So, it seems when I started to actually move forward in getting these books out, I needed a higher learning curve regarding destiny. I'm on the learn as you go plan and now I wonder if there is any other way?

May you be encouraged by my fumbling through my destiny publicly online and in books. Find your scroll, begin the journey of unlocking it with Yeshua, have your house judged, cross thresholds and rule as you are intended to in Him. We are a new creation and we have a whole new beginning, a new Jerusalem, a new heavens and a new earth - He makes all things new.

.

The End
And New Beginning…

IF YOU ENJOYED THIS BOOK

Please tell others! I would appreciate an honest review or simply click on a star rating, thanks.

Finding Your Destiny Scroll: Excerpts from a Discussion on Heavenly Scrolls and Mountains

Sharing from my journey and answering questions in a chat group style

---

Finding My Destiny Scroll: A Guidebook to Accessing Destiny

A progressive step by step guidebook with activations to help you connect with Jesus and engage your destiny scroll.

My Destiny Scroll: A Scribe's Record

A companion blank lined journal with artwork and scriptures for recording your journey

---

Judge My House: Destiny of a Bloodline

Sharing from my journey into judgment and the courts and government of our Father

ABOUT THE AUTHOR

Sheri Scott is an author and entrepreneur living in Calgary, Alberta, Canada, where she enjoys life with her husband, Noah, and her three teenaged children.

As a design thinker, she has continually sought a view of a bigger picture in the pursuit of her heavenly home, family and Father. She started SHARE Resources Inc., an innovation and idea company, to help facilitate the destinies of creative entrepreneurs. She is part of the creative team for the children's illustrated book series, The TRIA VIA Journals™ by Angela Thunket, also published by SHARE.

www.thetriaviajournals.com

Her desire is that everyone experience the grand adventure of understanding their destiny and journeying into our Father's house.

www.ingramcontent.com/pod-product-compliance
Lightning Source LLC
Chambersburg PA
CBHW071422070526
44578CB00003B/653